DATE DUE

BUTTERFLY

LIVING THINGS

BUTTERFLY

Rebecca Stefoff

BENCHMARK BOOKS

MARSHALL CAVENDISH
NEW YORK

Benchmark Books
Marshall Cavendish Corporation
99 White Plains Road
Tarrytown, New York 10591-9001

Illustrations by Jean Cassels

Library of Congress Cataloging-in-Publication Data
Stefoff, Rebecca
Butterfly / Rebecca Stefoff.
p.   cm. — (Living things)
Includes bibliographical references and index.
Summary: Introduces the life cycle and habitat of butterflies.
ISBN 0-7614-0413-9 (lib. bdg.)
1. Butterflies—Juvenile literature. [1. Butterflies.]
I. Title. II. Series: Stefoff, Rebecca, Living things.
QL544.2.S74   1997   595.78'9—dc21   96-46137   CIP   AC

Photo research by Ellen Barrett Dudley

Cover photo: *Peter Arnold, Inc.*, Darlyne A. Murawski

The photographs in this book are used by permission and through the courtesy of:
Peter Arnold, Inc.: Hans Pfletschinger, 2, 18 (left), 19 (left); Luiz C. Marigo, 8
(bottom left), 19 (right); John Cancalosi, 8 (bottom right); Alan Morgan, 11 (left);
Norbert Wu, 11 (right); Darlyne A. Murawski, 12, 18 (right); John Vucci, 13; IFA,
14; David Cavagnaro, 16; Kevin Schafer, 17; James L. Amos, 24; Martin Wendler, 26.
The National Audubon Society Collection/Photo Researchers, Inc.: Kjell B.
Sandved, 6–7, 13 (insert); John Mitchell, 8 (top left); Ray Coleman, 8 (top right);
Camazine/Trainer, 9; James H. Carmichael, Jr., 10; Stephen Dalton, 15; Tom
McHugh, 20; Scott Camazine, 21 (left & right); Pat Lynch, 22 (left, center & right);
Rod Planck, 23, 27; Gregory G. Dimijian, 25; John Bova, 32.

Printed in the United States of America

3   5   6   4   2

For Ilsa

blue morpho, Peru

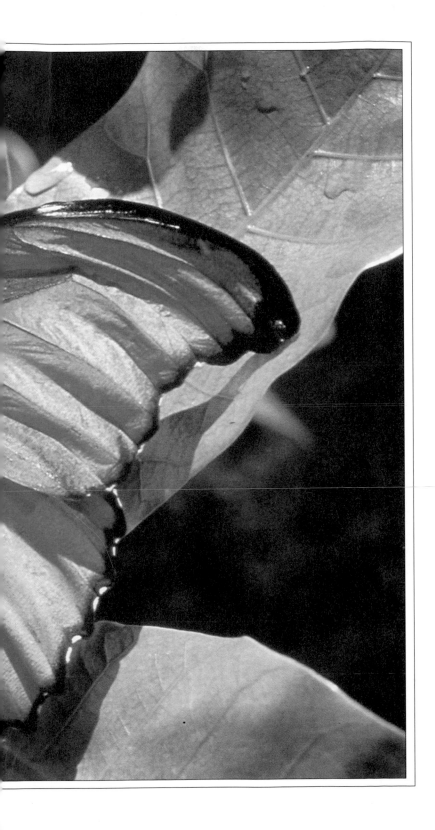

Has a piece of bright blue sky fallen down to the earth? Or is this a shining blue flower growing in the forest?

It's a butterfly. In a moment it may fly away on wings thinner than paper and as bright as a jewel.

tropical swallowtail   *swallowtail, Japan*

agrias butterfly, Brazil   *malachite butterfly, Costa Rica*

another swallowtail

Butterflies are insects, like ants and flies and bees. There are about seventeen thousand kinds of butterflies in the world. More different kinds live in the rain forests of South America than anywhere else on earth.

Some butterflies have names that tell what they look like. The tiger swallowtail has yellow and black stripes, like a tiger.

tiger swallowtail, North America

eighty-eight butterfly, South America

owl butterfly, South America

Guess which of these butterflies is called the owl butterfly. Here's a hint: its spots look like an owl's eyes. The other one is called the eighty-eight butterfly. Do you know why?

Butterflies live on nectar, the sweet juice inside flowers. The butterfly's mouth is a long, skinny tube. Most of the time the butterfly keeps its mouth tube neatly rolled up. When the butterfly lands on a juicy flower, it unrolls the tube. Then it sips the nectar through the tube, just as you sip milk through a straw.

See the bright blue scales like shingles on a roof? All butterflies' wings are covered with scales like these. The scales give butterflies their special colors.

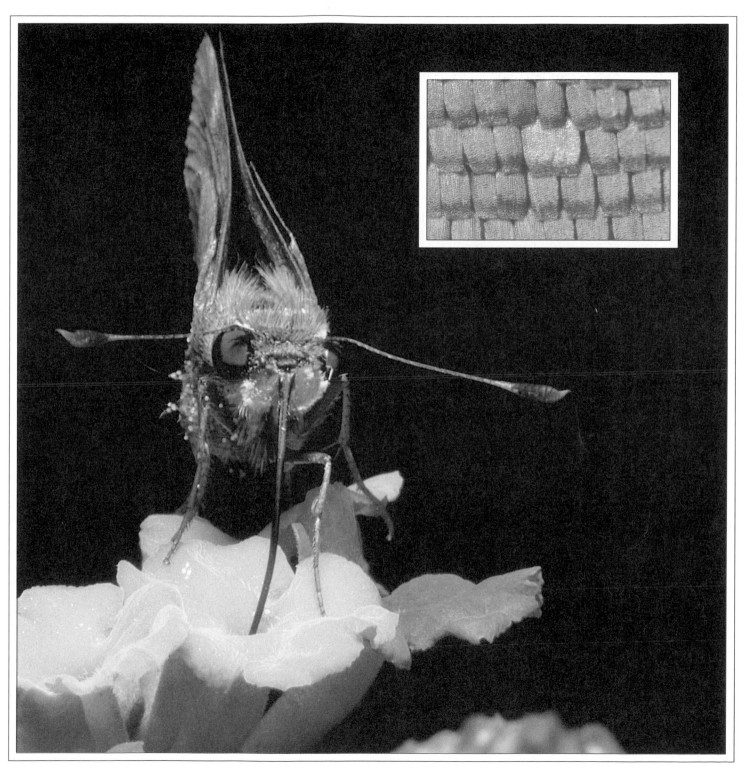

giant skipper feeding on flower nectar; with close-up of wing scales

Moths are cousins of butterflies. There are even more moths in the world than butterflies.

It's not easy to tell moths and butterflies apart. Even scientists can't always do it. But most butterflies fly by day, and most moths fly in the evening or at night. If something flutters by you as the sun goes down, it's probably a moth.

elephant hawk moth

emperor moths

imperial moth

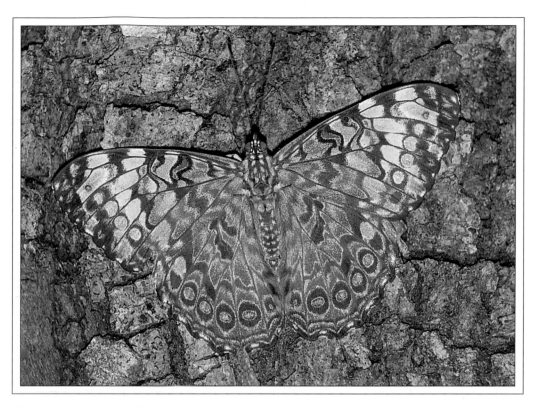

hamadrayas butterfly

Can you find the insects in these pictures? Even if *you* can find them, maybe a hungry bird or lizard can't.

Some moths and butterflies have special markings that help them hide in plants or on tree bark. If the butterfly or moth sits very, very still, that hungry bird or lizard will pass right by.

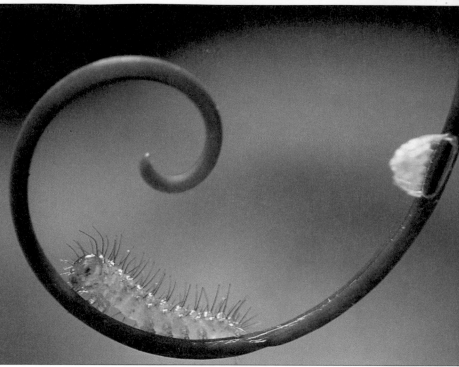

All butterflies and moths start life as tiny eggs. When the eggs hatch, stubby little creatures called caterpillars come crawling out. They start chomping on leaves. Each kind of caterpillar likes certain kinds of leaves.

Some caterpillars are tiny, not much bigger than a grain of rice. Some of them are big and bushy and brightly colored.

hawk moth caterpillar   *morpho butterfly caterpillars*

Caterpillars spend most of their time eating. But when it is time for them to move on to the next part of their lives, they stop eating.

Moth caterpillars make nests called cocoons. They weave the cocoons from fine, silky threads that come out of their bodies.

silkworm moth cocoons

monarch caterpillar turning into pupa   *monarch pupa*

A butterfly caterpillar doesn't spin a cocoon. Instead, it hangs from a leaf or branch and holds still. Slowly the caterpillar's skin turns into a hard shell, and the caterpillar becomes a quiet, resting thing called a pupa.

monarch pupa and emerging butterfly

Inside the shell, something wonderful is happening. The pupa is turning into a butterfly. When the butterfly is ready to come out, the shell of the pupa cracks open. Out comes a butterfly.

The first thing every new butterfly has to do is dry its wings. This new monarch butterfly has crawled onto a plant. Soon it will spread its wings for the very first time and let the sun dry them. Then it will be ready to fly.

monarch butterfly dries wings after leaving pupa

There's something special about the monarch butterfly. Every fall monarch butterflies from all over North America fly south for hundreds of miles. They always go to the same places in the mountains of Mexico. Millions of monarch butterflies gather there, until the trees are covered with the living, flickering fire of their wings.

monarchs on fall migration, Florida

millions of monarchs, Mexico

spectacled caiman with butterflies, Brazil

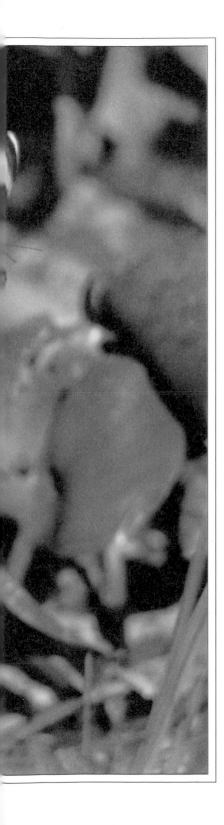

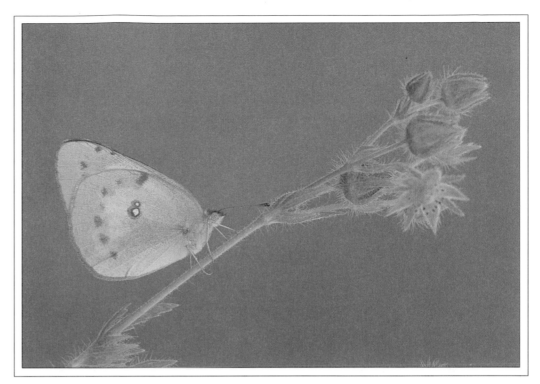

common sulphur butterfly, Michigan

You don't have to go deep into the jungle to see butterflies. Try looking for them in your neighborhood. Wherever there are flowers, there will be butterflies, too.

And the next time you see a crawling caterpillar, remember—some day it will be a butterfly.

A QUICK LOOK AT THE BUTTERFLY

Butterflies and moths belong to a large group of insects called Lepidoptera, which means "scale-wing." Scientists have identified one hundred seventy thousand kinds, or species, of Lepidoptera. About one-tenth of them are butterflies, and the rest are moths.

The name "butterfly" probably came from a species of Lepidoptera called the bright yellow brimstone. People in England called it the "butter-colored fly," and gradually the name came to be used for all butterflies.

Here are five kinds of butterflies and a moth along with their scientific names in Latin and a few key facts.

WESTERN PYGMY BLUE

Brephidium exilis   (breh FIH dee um ek ZYE liss)

One of the smallest known butterflies. Measures a half to three-fourths of an inch across (1.3–1.9 cm). Lives in wetlands and dry lowlands from the Southwestern United States through South America.

PURPLE EMPEROR

Apatura iris
(ah pah TOO rah EE ris)
Males are blackish-brown and metallic purple, with white markings; females have no purple. Measures three inches across (7.6 cm). Lives in woodlands from Europe to Japan. Caterpillar feeds on willow plants.

FIGTREE BLUE

Myrina silenus   (mee REE nah sigh LAY nus)
Measures about 1.5 inches across (3.8 cm). Lives in tropical forest and farmland throughout most of Africa. Caterpillar eats leaves of fig trees.

MADAGASCAN SUNSET MOTH

Chrysiridia riphearia
(krih sih RID ya rih FEER yah)
Lives only in Madagascar, an island off the coast of southern Africa. Measures four inches across (10 cm). Has been called the most beautiful of all moths. In 19th century, specimens were sent to England, where their wings were made into jewelry.

LONG-TAILED SKIPPER

Urbanus proteus
(ur BAY nus PRO tee us)
One of a large group of butterflies called skippers because they fly in a jumpy, skipping motion between flowers. Often seen in the United States as far north as Connecticut and California. Measures 1.5 to 2 inches across (3.8–5 cm).

29

QUEEN ALEXANDRA'S BIRDWING

Ornithoptera alexandrae   (orr nih THOP teh rah al ex AN dreye)
World's largest known butterfly. Males are bright blue-green, black, and yellow; about seven inches across (18 cm). Females are black and brown and much larger, up to eleven inches across (28 cm). Lives in rain forest of Papua New Guinea. Endangered species.

Taking Care of the Butterfly

Many butterflies and moths are vanishing from our world. When forests are cut down or meadows are turned into shopping malls, butterflies lose their homes and their food. Some zoos now have special "butterfly gardens" to help save these wonderful creatures, but we should also try to protect wilderness areas, so that butterflies can keep fluttering by in the places they have always lived. And you can invite butterflies to your yard or window box by planting wildflowers.

Find Out More

Butterfield, Moira. *Butterfly.* New York: Little Simon, 1992.

Hariton, Anita. *Butterfly Story.* New York: Dutton Children's Books, 1995.

Ryder, Joanne. *Where Butterflies Grow.* New York: Lodestar Books, 1989.

Terry, Trevor. *The Life Cycle of a Butterfly.* New York: Bookwright Press, 1988.

Whalley, Paul. *Butterfly and Moth.* New York: Knopf, 1988.

Index

Rebecca Stefoff has published many books for young readers. Science and environmental issues are among her favorite subjects. She lives in Oregon and enjoys observing the natural world while hiking, camping, and scuba diving.

great spangled fritillary